P9-DFW-779
Lineberger Memorial
Library
Lutheran Theological Southern Seminary Columbia, S. C.

The Cricket Winter

Bl. Eerd. 10/06 15.00

Originally published in 1967 by W. W. Norton

This edition published in 2006 by Eerdmans Books for Young Readers
an imprint of Wm. B. Eerdmans Publishing Company
255 Jefferson SE, Grand Rapids, MI 49503
P.O. Box 163, Cambridge CB3 9PU U.K.

www.eerdmans.com/youngreaders

06 07 08 09 10 11   6 5 4 3 2 1

Printed in the United States

Produced by Design Press,
a division of the Savannah College of Art and Design
www.designpressbooks.com
Design by Anna Marlis Burgard
Jacket type design by Judythe Sieck

Library of Congress Cataloging-in-Publication Data

Holman, Felice.
The cricket winter / written by Felice Holman; Illustrated by Robyn Thomas.— 1st ed.
p. cm.
Summary: A little boy exchanges Morse code messages with the cricket that lives in his house and together they trap the rat that has been plaguing the boy's father and the cricket's friends.
ISBN-10 : 0-8028-5289-0 / ISBN-13 : 978-0-8028-5289-2 (alk. paper)
[1. Crickets--Fiction. 2. Fantasy.] I. Thomas, Robyn, 1957- ill. II. Title.
PZ10.3.H727Cri 2006
[Fic]--dc22
2005032088

For those I love, with love — F.H.

* * *

For my parents — R.T.

Also by Felice Holman

Slake's Limbo
The Wild Children
Real
At the Top of My Voice and Other Poems
The Witch on the Corner
The Future of Hooper Toote
—and others

Felice Holman

Illustrated by Robyn Thomas

Eerdmans Books for Young Readers
Grand Rapids, Michigan / Cambridge, U.K.

Contents

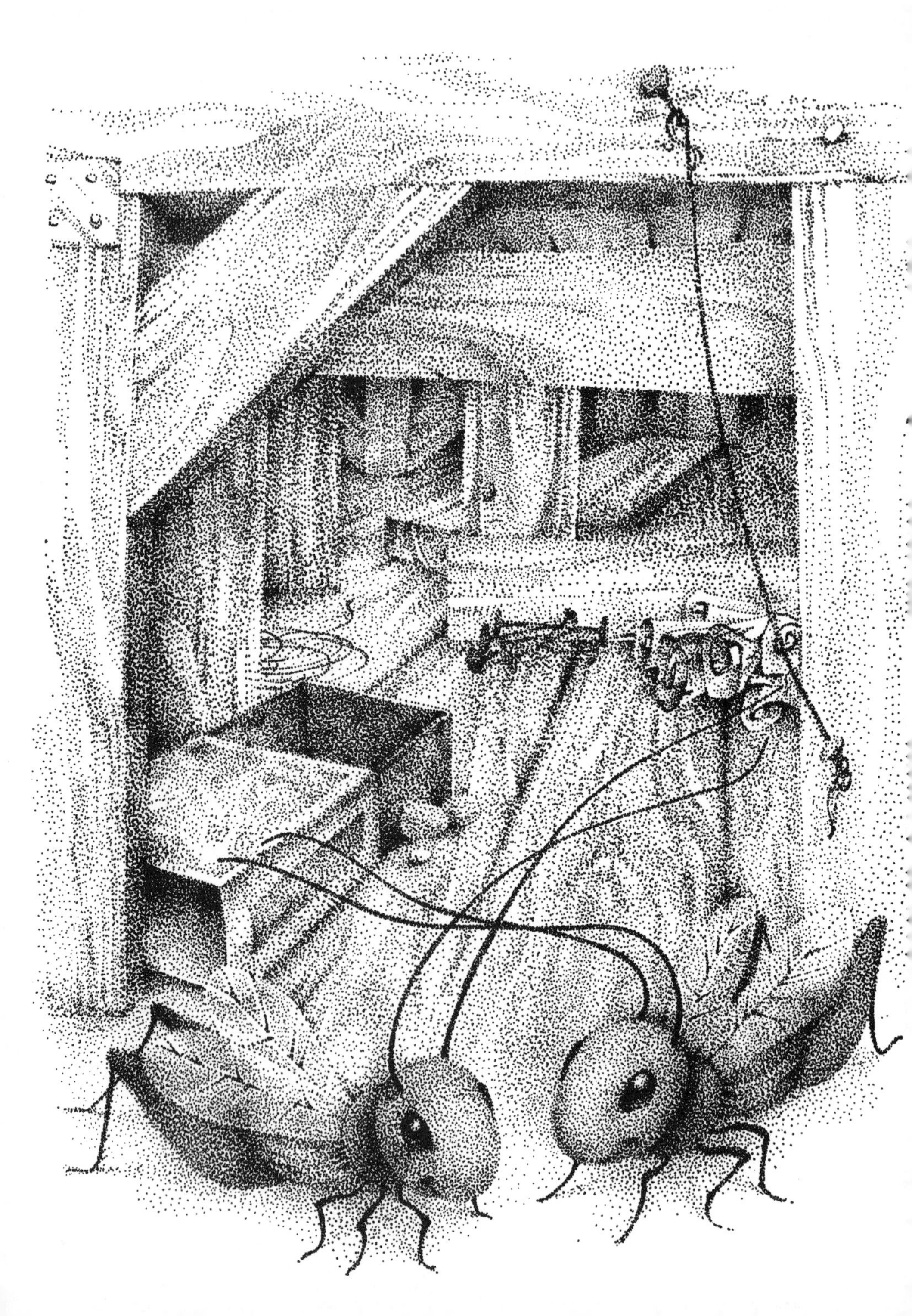

About the Cricket

A cricket is a delicate creature — one of the poetic things that nature has worked out — and a cricket-in-love is so tender and heart-rending, so attuned to his love, that he is, for the moment, at least, quite perfect.

A CERTAIN CRICKET, who had no special name, but was known simply (as are all crickets) as *Orthoptera Gryllidae*, having fallen in love, began to prepare a home for his future bride.

It was a superior place, being a space beneath the floor of an exceedingly snug house, indeed, so snug that the cricket himself had been able to find only one entrance to it, and this was a very small chink in an otherwise well-maintained foundation.

To call the cricket's new home a house is really not to say enough, because when one considers the relative size of house and cricket, it would be more nearly true to say it was a mansion. The ceilings were high; it was well ventilated, but warm; there were passages and chambers that were spacious and adaptable. Thus, in the late fall days, this cricket prepared a home for his love, and while he worked he sang incessantly.

Ah, well, tragedy can occur when it is least expected or deserved, and in most unlikely ways. The cricket and his love had a serious difference of opinion. It started with a disagreement about the rearing of the children that they hoped to have.

"We shall be very firm with them," the lady cricket had said, "kind, but firm. And lead them into paths of high moral behavior and great purpose." "But that's nonsense!" cried the cricket-in-love, for he was shocked — shocked and sad. "Cricket children are, by their very nature, free beings, independent! We must allow them to be free as . . . as crickets, to find their own purpose and principles."

"*No,*" said the lady. "Never! I have made up my mind to it. The trouble with you is that you are unrealistic. You don't see the seriousness of life. Well, I don't want my children to be like that!" And one strong word led to the dreadful next and the awful next, and the lady stamped her lovely foot and ran to her parents who had set up a winter home in the loft of the garage.

The cricket-in-love returned to his new home alone. Lonely, and with a great hurt in his heart, he mourned his lost love, and yet he could not bring himself to go to her. Perhaps it was the same with her.

And one night it snowed and sealed up, for the time being, the very small chink in the foundation.

About the Boy

A boy of nine is enormously wise and has a great deal to tell, if anyone at all would listen. And yet it is a fact that the ideas and opinions of many boys of nine are given very little notice or are entirely overlooked. Many adults who could learn from them, if they would, pass them by in a great hurry. It is not a perfect situation.

A CERTAIN BOY, whose name was Simms Silvanus (though he would have much preferred "John") probably knew more about polar exploration than his mother knew about baking, more about active volcanoes than his father knew about business, and more about electromagnets than anyone in his class. And much much more! He was inventive — he had ideas to improve things that would stagger you. And yet nobody listened! They interrupted before he had even nearly finished, or sometimes they pretended to listen but really they didn't hear anything. And yet surely the facts he had to tell were every bit as interesting as, for instance, a "sharp decline" in the stock market — something his father was speaking about before dinner, the particular night of the blow-up.

The *blow-up!* Possibly it might not have occurred if his mother had not made asparagus sauce. His father was very irritated, in the first place; there was this matter of the "sharp decline" (whatever *that* was!) and then there was the *rat*. His father had a more or less running battle with the rat. Mr. Silvanus had set countless traps, baited with all kinds of tempting things, all around the storeroom where he kept wild bird food and cracked corn for a small flock of pigeons. The rat made Mr. Silvanus absolutely furious.

"Got in again!" he said that night. "Tore open a brand new sack!" And with that, he took his first bite of the dinner that Mrs. Silvanus had set before him. "Clarissa!" he said then. "Canned asparagus soup is not really a sauce!"

"But you *like* asparagus soup," she replied.

"I like asparagus soup. I do not like asparagus soup sauce!"

Mrs. Silvanus looked hurt. "The magazine suggested it," she said. "*Ladies' Views*. They have very

good recipes. *They* said it was good on fish or poultry." And her voice was a bit like a spring wound too tight.

"I'm sorry I mentioned it," said Mr. Silvanus, and there followed a brief silence.

Simms sensed that there was time for him in this pause. "I'll tell you what," he said. "If you take a bunch of magnetic compasses and put them around a wire with current going through it — you know what happens?"

"Simms!" his father cried. "Just for tonight, let's not hear anything about magnetic fields and so forth!"

"But I didn't finish!" complained Simms.

"Finish another time, dear," his mother said.

"But listen, if you *reverse* the current, you know what happens?"

"Simms!" said his father. "I believe you heard me. Now go to your room for the rest of the evening."

One of the many charming things about crickets is that they do not sulk. They do not make others live through their personal tragedies. They rise above. They adjust. And a cricket-who-has-lost-his-love is not less perfect to the casual eye than a cricket-in-love. He alone knows that he is.

On the other hand, a boy who has lost, for the moment, the ear and the heart of his family, who has fallen from the sunny place to some dark hole where banished boys dwell, is inclined to sulk, to drag his feet, to smack about at feather pillows, and to wish desperately for some sympathetic companion — old in experience but young in heart — to understand him, to listen to him, and to love him just the way he is. Futile. All futile. And having sulked, and dragged, and smacked for as much time as it is worth, the boy is likely to look around the room for something to keep him busy during the evening of banishment.

Simms decided to build a telegraph key. It was a decision that would change things for the boy and for the cricket!

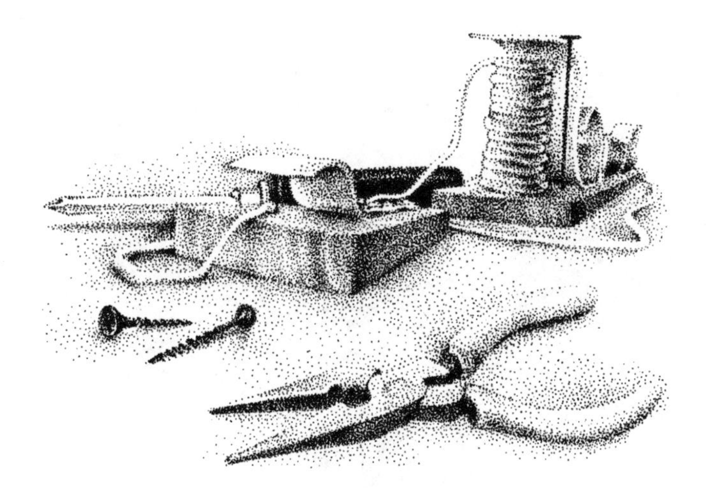

A Way of Speaking

IN THE FIRST WEEKS that Cricket had been living beneath the floor of Simms' house, he had been entirely alone with plenty of time to think and to adjust. And although he was lonely, he was quite comfortable. The warmth from the rooms above heated the space beneath the floor, and bits of curled wood shavings and small blocks of wood, left from the building of the house, made comfortable places to snug down, varied the decor, and some were even edible. But he missed his love sorely, and being a friendly creature, he missed companionship in general. That is why, when things grew brisk upstairs and voices were heard, the cricket would hop over under the room where the people were talking and pay strict attention.

The rise and fall of the voices, the inflections, the emphasis — all carried a kind of meaning to him, though the words themselves meant nothing at first. But the cricket's need was great, and it wasn't long before he could attach meaning to the recurring sounds and inflections, and by December the cricket was beginning to understand something about the life going on in the rooms above him. Some of the problems were entirely familiar. Some were quite strange.

He heard the irritation of the father — his worry and concern, his annoyance about the rat. He heard the endearing reassurances of the mother, and the restlessness of the boy. And, he heard the endless notions that the boy propounded. There was a grand scheme to build a covered bridge across the snowdrifts, to avoid the constant shoveling that was a bothersome chore for his father. (The boy's father gave very little attention to that idea.) There was another great idea — a pot-stirrer. "I can attach a big spoon to an arm that would be attached to the turntable of my record player," Simms had said to his mother. "It could stir the pot for you while you do something else." (His mother had rejected the idea . . . but with thanks.)

And then, one night — it was a few nights after a lively discussion about asparagus sauce — the boy began to talk in a language that was much easier for the cricket to understand. It was, as a matter of fact,

A Rat Revealed

It is easy to suppose that the world one lives in, at the moment, is the whole world or the only world. And so the boy, accustomed as he was to the limits of his life, did not for a moment consider that there was a world beneath the house, inhabited by the cricket.

The cricket, for his part, while he knew of the world above, was quite unaware that there was even more life in the house beneath him.

ONE EVENING CRICKET was relaxing beneath Simms' room, listening to the telegraph key, when suddenly there was a rush off to his left and then a furry, unkempt creature, whom the cricket recognized as a rat, came barreling through the cricket's apartment, knocking over neat piles of shavings, stirring up dust from insulating fibers, and generally disrupting the order and quiet.

The cricket was surprised and annoyed, but more than that, he was interested. "For goodness

sake!" he thought. "I never saw *him* before! I didn't know there was another soul down here." And then he thought, "I'll just see where he goes," and abandoning the lesson in Morse code, he followed the rat, hopping and creeping from beam to rafter, from rafter to beam, as the rat ran along ahead of him.

The route followed along under the first-floor rooms of the house and then dropped suddenly downward, between the studs of two walls, and into a dark basement where the furnace was. As the rat came out into the basement he hesitated, looked right and left like a man crossing a railroad track, muttered something like "Aha!" and then darted into a corner behind the furnace itself. The cricket waited a moment and then followed. He was wary . . . not in the least eager to find himself in a dark corner with the rat. But his curiosity and loneliness were strong, and he crept behind the furnace. There was not a sign of the rat.

Cricket was perplexed. "There's absolutely nowhere else he could have gone," he mused. "This is the only way to get behind the furnace, and I would have seen him if he had come out. He has to be in here." And so he started a careful investigation, creeping over every inch of the basement floor, and finally starting up the stone foundation wall. And then he found it! One of the rocks of the foundation protruded from the wall just enough to conceal what seemed to be a small cave. The cricket peered in. It was so dark that it was impossible to see more than an inch, but he courageously put his head in. The rat was not there, but the opening now seemed less a cave than a tunnel, and from the other end of it came voices. They were not people voices; they were animal voices. The lonely cricket stepped into the tunnel.

It was only a short passage, a bit curvy, and the depth of the foundation wall — eighteen inches perhaps — but it was quite a nerve-racking eighteen inches for a cricket in the dark, in the damp, in the cold, and with who-knows-what on the other side. As he reached the end of the tunnel the cricket moved slowly, ready to retreat in a hurry, if need be. He crouched low on the tunnel floor and put his head carefully out the opening on the other side of the wall.

And what a pleasant surprise! Instead of any number of expected horrors, a rather pleasant domestic scene greeted him — a sort of encampment or compound, one might say, inhabited by several familiar creatures.

Where the cricket had finally emerged was a small, shallow cellar beneath the sun porch. Its floor was of earth — part of the same gently sloping bank that made up the garden around the house. The walls were the stone foundation walls of the house and porch, and the low roof was of wood, being the under side of the sun porch floor. It seemed quite comfortable and dry, except for a small puddle in one corner; however, the temperature of the air was generally cooler than the cricket liked.

From where he crouched in the tunnel entrance, a few inches above the floor, the cricket had an excellent view. To his left, along the western wall of the cellar, a mouse family had made its home, and a very comfortable home it seemed to be. The mother was at that moment bedding down her several children in little beds made of bits of cloth and straw, arranged in the low rafters of the porch.

The father mouse was just that minute arriving in the cellar from a small hole in the far corner. He climbed up into the rafters and added a few sunflower seeds to a neat supply that was arranged in what seemed to be the larder. There were other things in the larder — indistinguishable dried bits that were, no doubt, appetizing to mice. It was a tidy, cozy house. When he had finished arranging the food supply, the father mouse descended to the living area and just paced back and forth.

In the near left-hand corner, not far from the puddle, an enormous family of ants was hurrying about in the way that ants are always hurrying — errands, errands, errands, as though there were no end to them. And, indeed, there was not, because it took all their efforts to keep so complicated a household running. An apartment of many rooms was concealed in the foundation wall and an underground entrance to it emerged in the dirt floor of the compound. In the wall the ants carried on a busy, serious, and civilized life.

Across the compound and framed like a statue in a niche, a mole slept in the wall. She looked as though she had been built there, so perfect was the fit. It was, in fact, a pure accident — her being there — since her own long tunnel under the ground had ended there quite by chance.

Above her, a spider web stretched across the rafters in the corner. A large spider rested in the center of the web.

At the moment, the rat was making his lumbering way across the dirt floor. He was bragging as he approached the mouse family. "They've set two traps now — one high, one low. Even a fool could see them; and I'm no fool." He swaggered and shook himself, and mussed up his already mussed and dirty fur. "I found a bag of juicy potatoes, and a safe new route back!"

"Where? How?" asked the father mouse.

"Hah!" was all the rat said. And then he shook himself again and dragged his feet as he walked across the packed earth floor, making tracks in a part of the compound that the mother mouse had just tidied up that evening. Then he plunked himself down on his very scrambled unmade bed of rags, and started to snore immediately. Now, the curious thing is that this bed was directly in front of and under the tunnel entrance.

It is possible that no one has ever attempted to count, but the number of mice in the world is enormous, and every single one is named *Mus*. It is very confusing, and the only thing for a mouse to do, to keep his individuality, is to act as if he were the only one named *Mus*. This is what Mr. and Mrs. Mus did, and, in truth, they and their children were the only Musses in that particular house — except for the rat. Because, as a matter of cold fact, rats are also called *Mus*, but the mouse family, without actually denying it, never admitted it. They called him Hostis.

"That Hostis is a real rat!" said Mrs. Mus disgustedly, sweeping up the rat tracks with her tail. "*A real rat!*" And the cricket could tell that this was not a compliment. Cricket now edged carefully out of the tunnel, crept past the rat with the light quiet steps of a cricket and made his way across the stone wall to a place near the mouse home. Then he said very softly, "Good evening?" And it turned out to be a sort of question.

Mrs. Mus looked up from her sweeping. "Evening," she said. And Mr. Mus came and stood beside her.

"I didn't realize you were down here," said Cricket. "I'm way over on the other side of the house, you see." He waved in the general direction. "Over that way. Some distance."

"Ah," said Mr. Mus.

"You've got quite a group here," said the cricket, and he was so lonely he may have said it enviously . . . even though the chill air would not have been right for him.

"Yes," said Mrs. Mus. "Quite a group! Especially that Hostis!"

"Who?" asked Cricket.

"Hostis, that rat."

"Oh," said the cricket.

"He's a rat," said Mrs. Mus, "a real rat—and dirtier than most, and greedier than most, and more selfish and self-centered than most . . . and . . ."

"There, there!" Mr. Mus tried to soothe her. "Don't get so upset." But Mrs. Mus began to cry.

"You'll have to excuse her," said Mr. Mus. "She's worried about the food supply because of the snow. You see," he looked over his shoulder at the sleeping rat, "Hostis has claimed all rights to the food supply in the house. You can see how he sleeps near the tunnel? He didn't notice you because you're small and light-footed, but if we were to try and sneak past him there would be a terrible row — or worse."

"Say it! Say it!" Mrs. Mus cried. "He's even threatened to *kill* us!"

Mr. Mus patted her gently. "But fortunately," he went on with some pride, "I have a very good private tunnel, in the corner, that comes out in a very well hidden place under some bushes. Most of the time I can go through the tunnel and then scoot across the yard to get the food that blows off the bird feeder. The trouble is . . ."

"The trouble is," sobbed Mrs. Mus, "there's been so much snow this winter and such a hard freeze that sometimes the tunnel is blocked and frozen over for days at a time. Then we have to live very frugally on what we have stored."

"The seeds I brought home tonight," said Mr. Mus, "were just a few I managed to find on the floor of the tunnel. It's frozen quite solid now. There's plenty to be had in the house and shed, but the rat won't let us near it. And he *is* bigger . . ."

"And bolder!" said Mrs. Mus, a trifle critically.

"Yes," said Mr. Mus ruefully. "I'll admit it. He is bolder than I am. Why, he'll go through places that are simply lined with traps, and miss them all! He seems to know where they'll put them next. He's not stupid; I'll say that for him."

"Well," said Cricket, because it seemed to be his turn to say something, "I'm sorry to hear of your trouble. I am. I wish I could help you." (It was not the last time he would say that.)

"Well," said Mr. Mus, suddenly cheerful, "it's not all black, you know. No, indeed! Where would we be without water? I ask you that. But are we short of water? No. That's the answer. 'Why?' you may ask." He looked sharply at the cricket.

"Why?" asked the cricket.

"Because," said Mr. Mus, "we selected this cellar with an eye to its excellent water supply — the fortunate leak that you see off to your right." And he pointed to the puddle that Cricket had noticed when he entered the compound. "One of the roof drains is wrong or something, and we've always had a very nice water hole there." He looked at Mrs. Mus to see if this had cheered her, but if it had, it was not noticeable. "You'll feel better after a good night's sleep," he said to her. "Things look better in the morning."

"Forgive me," said the cricket. "I'm keeping you up. It's been a pleasure to meet you."

"Come again," said Mrs. Mus, forgetting her worries long enough to remember her manners. "Come soon. We'd be pleased."

"So would I," said Cricket. And he meant it.

A Voice from Below

IT SNOWED AGAIN for a whole day and a night, and the paths that Mr. Silvanus had dug to the road, and out to the garbage cans, and to the garage, were quite covered again. Schools were closed. It was not an unwelcome holiday for Simms, although he missed his school friends. But, if the truth were known, it really was a relief, for a change, to be free of the sound of his teacher's voice — dotted with "i's," crossed with "t's," and sprinkled with commas and semicolons.

Simms had a good deal of time to do what he wished. He swept up the kitchen for his mother and sorted out all the old nails and screws for his father and put them into separate boxes. Then he put together a jigsaw puzzle. He read three chapters in *Swiss Family Robinson* and began to think a warm climate might be nicer after all, even if there wasn't any snow to roll in. Then he lay on his back on the bed and stared out the window. What he saw was a glaring white patch of world through looped white organdy curtains. It was beautiful, but it just wasn't enough. Simms got up and went to his telegraph key.

He did a few trial runs of letters and punctuation marks, just as a sort of exercise. Then he decided that he was ready for words. That wasn't so easy, but he went at it slowly. "Hello," tapped Simms. "Hello." He thought that was probably a good way to start a message. So he practiced that several times. "Hello. My name is Simms." Very good! "My name is Simms," he tapped again. "I am a boy. I am a boy of nine." He thought that he was doing quite well for a beginner. It was slow, but it was accurate. "What a shame this isn't hooked up," he thought. "It's too bad someone doesn't have a set I could send messages to. When this snow stops, I'm going to see if I can get one of my friends to learn." And then he tapped again. "Hello. My name is Simms." He was really getting the hang of it. "Hello. My name is Simms. I am a boy of nine." And then, in the pause that followed, *there came an answer!*

"Hello," came a piping sound in Morse code. Simms' hand hung in the air over the telegraph key. It was hard to believe, and yet it *did* seem to be an answer.

"But it's not connected to anything! There's no one receiving the message," he mused. "How could it be? I must have imagined it, or maybe it was just an echo." But he tried again. "Hello!" he tapped.

"Hello," came the creaky answer.

Simms' hand was unsteady, but he rushed as much as he could. "I'm Simms," tapped Simms.

There was a pause, and then slowly, uncertainly, but at the same time unmistakably, came the chirped reply. "I'm *Orthoptera Gryllidae.*"

Simms' mind churned, and as quickly as he could, he tapped out, "Who did you say you are? And where are you, anyhow?"

Slowly, too, but gaining in skill, the reply was chirped. "*Orthoptera Gryllidae*. Cricket." And then again. "*Orthoptera Gryllidae*. Cricket. Underneath the floor. Underneath the floor."

Simms discovered that it was even harder to listen to a message than to send one, but he worked hard and fast to try and understand. When he had thought it out he still couldn't believe it.

He mulled it over in his mind for a bit, and after a few moments he came to a conclusion that was partly true. "For heaven's sake!" he thought. "Crickets understand Morse code! I wonder if anyone knows that? My word! It may be a discovery! That must be what they're doing all the time out in the fields all summer — dots and dashes!" He got back to the key.

"Hello," he tapped, because he could do that very fast by now.

"Hello," chirped Cricket.

"How are things?" tapped Simms.

"What things?" asked the cricket.

Simms considered this. Then he tapped, "The things that have to do with your life. How are they?"

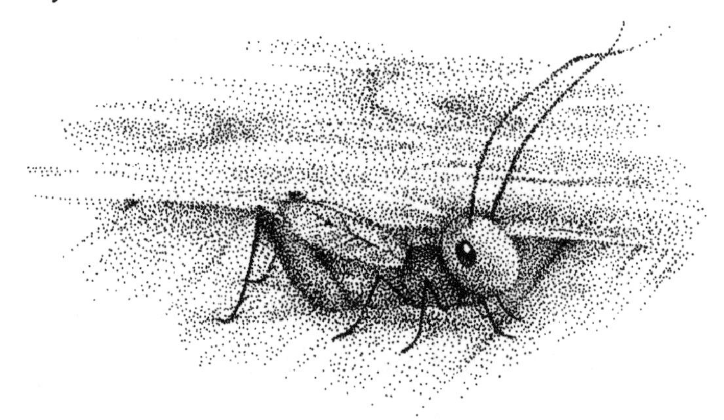

"That will take a lot of thought to answer precisely and fully, but I will think about it," chirped the cricket. "How are your things?"

Simms, who would have been able to answer this question a minute ago by saying "Just great," now answered slowly. "I will think about it, too." And so he phrased another question that was more particular. "Are you alone?"

"No," chirped Cricket. "And yes," he added. "I am

alone as a cricket, but as a creature I am not alone."

"Who is with you?" tapped Simms, and it must be understood that he tapped very slowly. However, the cricket, though he could chirp quickly, used the language slowly, so it was quite an even match.

"Right here, I am by myself," chirped Cricket. "However, on the other side of the house there are quite a few very pleasant folk — a mouse family, quite charming, he, she, and four young Mus children."

Simms was interested. "Mice!" he said. "My father would be wild. Do you know anything about a rat?"

"Yes," said Cricket. "There is one rat."

"Just one?"

"Just one."

"Big?"

"Enormous!"

"Who else is there?" asked Simms.

"There's a mole, a spider, and a very large group of ants."

"All in our house?" tapped Simms. "All these creatures live in our house?"

"All under the house," chirped Cricket.

"Tell me about them," tapped Simms.

"I've just met them," chirped Cricket. "I don't know them well, but the mice seem a bit anxious."

"About what?" tapped Simms. And at that moment a voice could be heard by both boy and cricket. It was a mother's voice saying, "Bedtime, Simms."

"I'll have to go now," tapped Simms hurriedly. But tell me tomorrow. Good night."

"A very good night," chirped Cricket.

Generally speaking, crickets do not get excited. They live a courteous and interested, but unexceptional life, and seldom are moved to enormous enthusiasms except, of course, in love. But that is among themselves. This particular cricket now sensed an unaccustomed feeling under his crisp coat of chitin. It was excitement.

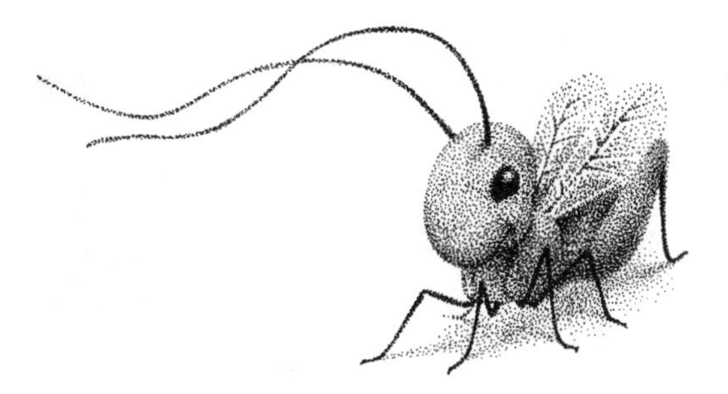

Trouble in the Compound

WHEN HE HAD RESTED and had a light snack, Cricket hurried across the beams and rafters, down the masonry wall, and into the basement. He paused and looked carefully into the cellar before he scooted into the space behind the furnace. Then he entered the tunnel.

When he emerged on the other side, a strange and somehow awesome sight greeted him. Grouped around in the center of the compound were all the inhabitants of the basement — all, except the Mus offspring, who were sleeping, and Hostis, the rat.

They were in a circle and they were talking in tense voices, so low that the cricket could not hear what they were saying. He inched in and came close to the circle. Mr. Mus was the first to notice him.

"Ah," he said. "Glad you could come," and his voice was serious. "You know everyone here." The cricket nodded a reserved and somewhat timid greeting.

"I hope I'm not intruding," he said. "I remembered your kind invitation to return. If this is a bad time . . ."

"A very bad time," said the mole in a deep, sad, and very sleepy voice.

"Ah, well, I'm sorry," said the cricket and started to back away from the circle.

"No, no!" said Mr. Mus. "Not a bad time for you to come — as a matter of fact, a good time for you to come — but the mole means a bad time for us all here in the compound. We have come upon a bad time, if you see what we mean."

"Yes," said Cricket. "I understand. But what is the trouble?"

"It's that Hostis!" cried Mrs. Mus, tears coming to her eyes. "He has become intolerable. My babies . . . my children . . . they went to bed tonight with scarcely a thing to eat!"

"Hostis has robbed us!" said Mr. Mus gravely. "Came right in and raided our larder!"

"It would be bad enough under ordinary circumstances," said the mole, sounding bored (but it must be remembered that moles are meant to be hibernating in winter, and she was not entirely alert). "Under ordinary circumstances," she said again, as though she had lost track of what she wanted to say. "Under ordinary circumstances . . . oh, yes! But, you see, at the moment, you see, the mouse tunnel to the outside of the house is . . . is . . ."

"The mouse tunnel is blocked with snow," said the spider, impatiently finishing the sentence for the mole.

"They can't get out, you see," said Chief Ant.

"They can't get any more food until it thaws. It's too bad. We're all concerned," and he waved at the other ants who nodded in agreement. "I can't help noticing, though," he said to Mr. Mus, "that you were not too well organized against this emergency. You did not have nearly enough put by. Not nearly enough."

Mrs. Mus, who had said just about the same thing not long ago, now spoke defensively. "He had a marvelous store of sunflower seeds. Marvelous!"

"Even if I'd had more, Hostis would have stolen them," said Mr. Mus.

"You could have protected your larder better," said Chief Ant. "We have ours barricaded, I can tell you that."

The ants all nodded. The cricket felt that under the circumstances Chief Ant was being a bit offensive, but he said nothing.

The mole opened her eyes. "He doesn't steal anything from me, because I'm on a diet in the winter. There's nothing to steal. But I just can't stand the way he litters the place. This is my sleeping room, after all!" And that seemed to remind her that she was sleepy. "Couldn't we get this over with? I want to get back to bed."

"Well, what do you think about it, as an objective observer?" asked Mr. Mus, looking at Cricket.

"Me?" asked Cricket. "Me?"

"Yes," said Mrs. Mus. "How does it sound to you?"

The cricket felt that this was an altogether unusual evening. Two very difficult questions had been asked of him and he was not used to such questions, nor of searching for the answers. Not only that, the air in the basement was chilly, and as crickets become cold, their speech becomes much slower. It is an odd fact, but a true one. On the hottest days, crickets speak quite fast — but the colder it gets, the slower they chirp. So now Cricket said, slowly, "It sounds quite sad. It sounds as though . . ."

"My word!" said the spider. "Are you going to fall asleep while you talk, like the mole?"

"No," said Cricket, apologetically. "I'm not tired, just a bit cold."

"Oh dear!" said Mrs. Mus. "You mustn't take a chill. Come over between Mr. Mus and me. We'll keep you warm." So the cricket hopped over between the Musses and snuggled in between them. Their soft fur made a comfortable robe for him and warmed him considerably.

"Now then," said Chief Ant. "You were saying that we ought to take some action."

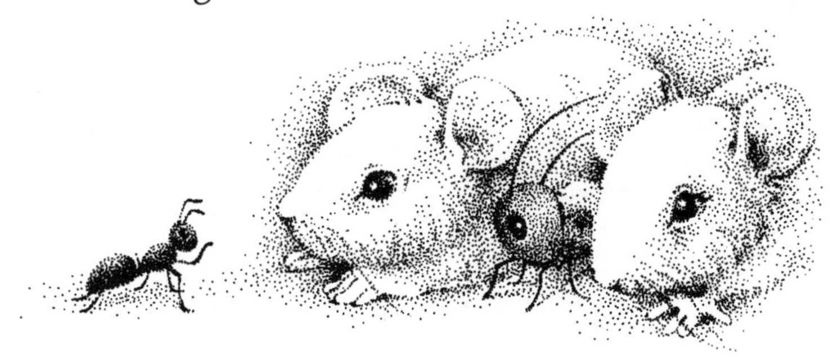

"Did I?" asked Cricket, somewhat muffled in fur. "I don't recall . . ."

"And you're right," said Chief Ant. All the other ants nodded. "Because it is only a matter of time before that rat tries to break into our house to get into our mushroom room."

"Mushroom room?" said Cricket.

"We raise them," said Chief Ant, and all the other ants nodded.

"But we've tried taking action," said Mrs. Mus.

"What sort of action?" asked Cricket.

"We tried freezing him out," said Mrs. Mus.

"Ignoring him," said the spider.

"Making him feel rejected," said Chief Ant.

"And what happened?" asked the cricket.

"He didn't even notice it," said Mrs. Mus. "Didn't even notice it."

At that moment there was a rustle at the entrance to the compound and the rat's head appeared in the tunnel entrance. His manner was sullen. "Couldn't get near the storeroom again," he said. "That man had a ring of traps. Very clever! But I'll outsmart him. All the same I'm hungry." And with a truculent shrug, he trudged right over to the

entrance of the ant apartment and then barged into the mouse quarters, knocking over everything and picking up the few remaining sunflower seeds.

"You rat!" screamed Mrs. Mus, and cried bitterly. But Hostis appeared not to hear her. He ambled shamelessly through the Mus home, waking the children, then shuffled off across the compound to his own slovenly hovel where he threw himself down onto the untidy pile of rags that he called a bed, and fell asleep immediately.

Mrs. Mus ran to tuck the children back into bed, and the oldest child, Young Mus, questioned her closely. "Why does he come in here like that?"

"Because he's a rat," said Mrs. Mus. "Because he couldn't get any food upstairs and so he takes ours. Because he's bigger." Young Mus thought it over as he fell back to sleep. Mrs. Mus rejoined the conference.

The conversation in the middle of the compound was resumed in lowered tones after the rat fell asleep. "Well," said the spider. "You see how it is! Now, what do you have to say?" He was addressing the cricket.

"Well," said Cricket, "since you ask me — and I should never have volunteered it if you hadn't— I do not think that rat is sensitive to hints and suggestions. I should simply go to him, and say outright, 'Look here,' or words to that effect. 'Look here,' I would say, 'we are going to ask you, quite directly, to tidy up and be considerate, and most particularly, to stop stealing and become community-minded, or we shall be forced to . . . er . . . exclude you from the community.'"

Mr. Mus looked doubtful, and the mole snorted. But Mrs. Mus said, "We could try it. It sounds decent. Try it," she said to Mr. Mus. "Go on."

"What, me?" he asked.

"Certainly, you," said the spider.

"What, now?" asked Mr. Mus.

"Right now," said Mrs. Mus. "If we don't do it now, we might never do it at all. Go on!"

"Oh, all right," agreed Mr. Mus, and looking nervously back at the group for support, he walked slowly across the compound to the rat's hovel. Mr. Mus gave the rat a gentle prod. The rat snorted and turned over, and Mr. Mus jumped back a few feet, but the rat slept on. Mr. Mus approached once more, and delivered a stronger prod. The rat opened his eyes and squinted up at Mr. Mus. Mr. Mus held his breath and seemed to forget his mission.

"Look here . . ." prompted Mrs. Mus in a hiss from across the compound.

"Look here," said Mr. Mus, and his voice could scarcely be heard, even by himself. "Look here," he said, a bit louder, marshaling his courage, "either you are to tidy up yourself, and your possessions, and your abode, and show some consideration and respect for the rights and property of others, and improve your moral outlook . . . or you will be ostracized!"

"*Ostracized!*" echoed the spider.

The rat stared at Mr. Mus. "Did you wake me up to tell me that?" he asked roughly.

"Yes," said Mr. Mus. "Yes, I did. That's precisely why I woke you up."

"Talk about consideration!" said the rat. "Well, push off! *Off!*" And he turned over with his back to one and all.

"There!" said Mr. Mus as he returned to the conference. "There, you see! He's hopeless!"

"You really can't approach him on any reasonable grounds at all," moaned the mole. "He's just so wrapped up in himself that he doesn't look to the right or to the left."

"Except if there's something of someone else's to take," sobbed Mrs. Mus.

"We may just have to put up with him," said Chief Ant, backing down from his aggressive stand. The other ants nodded. "We can't freeze him out. We can't intimidate him. And how are you going to ostracize him? I ask you that! No, we shall have to go on tolerating him."

"That's perfectly easy for you to say," said Mr. Mus, "because you are not getting the worst of it."

"He's walked right over our entrance more than once," said Chief Ant. "It's hard to bear. But I don't really see a solution."

"There may be one," said the spider thoughtfully. "There just *may* be one."

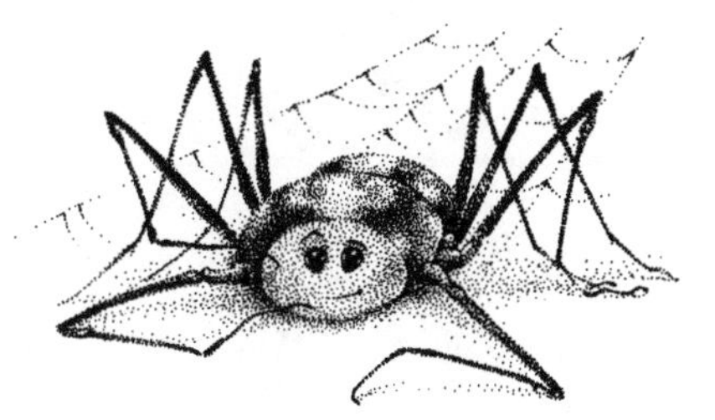

"What?" cried Mrs. Mus.

"Well, I'll think it over, and tell you at our meeting tomorrow, when he goes out." The spider addressed the cricket. "Will you be able to join us?"

"I'd be pleased to," said Cricket. "I wish there was something I could do. I really do."

Crickets are, not unlike everyone else, moved by the tragedy of others. They wish, oh, they wish to help! And sometimes their wish, and the wishes of others, and the forces of time and circumstance move them to do great acts. And it is not always the act they had wished to do when they were only vaguely wishing.

Cricket Reports

It snowed all that night and all the next morning. Even Mrs. Silvanus was beginning to worry a bit about keeping the larder full. "I'm afraid the bread's a bit dry," she said at supper the next night, "and the milkman couldn't get through."

"It's all right," said Mr. Silvanus. "We'll just make do with what we have."

Simms, surprisingly, said very little at supper that night and could hardly wait for the meal to be over. He helped clear the table, then rushed to his room and closed the door. He sat down and put his hand on the telegraph key. "Calling Cricket," he tapped. "Calling Cricket."

Cricket had been every bit as eager as Simms to talk again. As a matter of fact, he had been waiting under Simms' room for quite a while. Just how long is hard to say exactly.

"Calling Cricket."

"Cricket here," came the immediate, chirped reply.

"Simms here," Simms tapped. "How are things?"

The cricket was ready for the question this time. "There is a great deal to be said about that," he chirped. "Some of it is quite personal and I will not tire you with it."

"It won't tire me," tapped Simms.

"I believe, however," chirped Cricket, "I can sum up by saying that I, myself, have all the necessities of life, except one. Things are all right. It is not true, however, for everyone. How are your things?"

"Well, I have problems," tapped Simms. "I have great ideas, and no one cares. No one listens."

"I will listen," said Cricket.

"Then I will tell my ideas to you," tapped Simms. "But first, tell me about the mice."

"Their things are bad," chirped Cricket. "They're in trouble."

"What kind of trouble?" tapped Simms, as fast as he could.

"It's the rat," creaked Cricket.

"The rat!" tapped Simms. "What about the rat?"

"He is a threat to the community," said Cricket. "He has always been sullen and greedy, but now he steals from the mice, and they have very little for their children to eat these snowy days."

"It's the same here," said Simms. "The milkman couldn't come."

"The mouse tunnel to the outside is blocked and they can't go out to get food. Their children were hungry tonight," said the cricket.

Simms had one of his great ideas. "I could leave crumbs for them in the kitchen," said Simms. "My father would be furious, but I could do it."

"They can't come,"

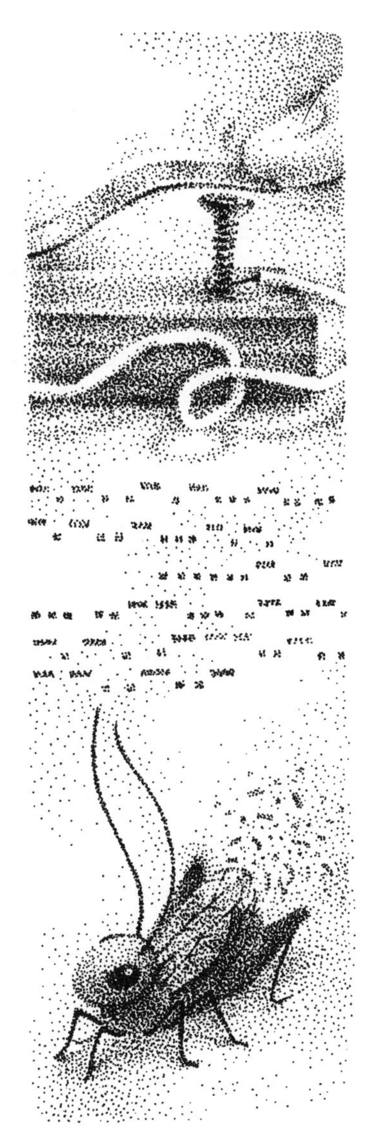

said Cricket. "The rat claims first rights. He won't let them come. You would just be feeding the rat."

"Well, we have to do something," said Simms.

"Everyone is working on the problem," said Cricket. "The mole, the spider, the ants, and the mice, of course. They are all working on it."

"So is my father," tapped Simms. "He sets traps."

"I've heard so," chirped the cricket. "I hear he is quite clever."

"Oh, yes, my father is very clever," tapped Simms, and he felt quite proud to hear that his father's reputation was so well known. "Are you going to see them all again soon?"

"Yes," said Cricket. "I have an appointment for later tonight, after the rat goes out."

"But what can they do?" asked Simms. What can a mole, and some ants, and a spider, and some mice do?"

"Just the best they can," chirped Cricket. "That's all they can do."

"Tell me tomorrow," tapped Simms.

"Yes," chirped Cricket. "Yes, I will tell you."

"Good night now," tapped Simms.
"A very good night," chirped the cricket.

The Meeting

Crickets do not count time the way people do. For example, a warm day is a certain length of time, but a cold day is a much longer time. For a cricket, supper with his love is a relatively short time, but supper alone is a very long time. And so on. This leads to a rather inexact time system by human standards, but it does not upset crickets.

THE CRICKET HAD A SHORT NAP after his long supper and awoke with a sense that the time for something was at hand. With all the excitement of the last few days — meeting the folk in the basement, talking with Simms — he was a little disoriented. It took him a moment to straighten out his thoughts and then . . . "The meeting!" he remembered, and hurried as fast as he could along the now familiar route to the basement.

He was late, but that is not surprising when one recalls the cricket's problem of reckoning time. The meeting was well under way as he arrived in the compound, and he approached the group quietly.

The mole was just finishing a speech. ". . . And what affects me most deeply," she was saying, "is that it is possible to be a rat without feeling remorse."

"How do you know he does not feel remorse? Perhaps he hides it well," said Cricket. And then he said, "Do forgive me for butting in."

"Not at all," said Mrs. Mus. "We're delighted you could come."

"Remorse doesn't have to he spoken," said the mole in her slow, slow voice. "Remorse can be seen and felt — in eyes, in voices, and even in sleep. A remorseful creature does not look like the rat does when he is asleep."

"It is because there is no love in him," said Mrs. Mus. "No love at all."

Cricket considered this idea, but he did not reply.

"So then, I take it we have decided," said Mr. Mus, who seemed to be acting as moderator of the meeting. Everyone nodded solemnly.

"Decided what?" asked Cricket.

"A great deal has gone on at this meeting before you arrived," said Mr. Mus.

"Yes," said the spider, letting himself down on a slender thread from a low beam, "we have decided to do away with him."

"Decided *what!*" exclaimed the cricket.

"To do away with him," said Chief Ant.

"To kill him," said Mrs. Mus.

"Kill him!" cried Cricket, looking from one to the other.

"Thoroughly!" said the mole.

Cricket felt the chill of the cellar again. His voice became slower. "No," he cried. "No. Don't do it!" And as he said it, he wondered if life was going on like this all the time, and he not aware of it. His own life was only the pleasure of the grass

and fields, the chorus of crickets, the warmth of his winter home, the love of his love . . . and the loneliness of his loneliness. “No! Don’t kill him!”

Mrs. Mus spoke to him kindly. “I know how you feel,” she said, “but it is the only way. There is no other way at all to make him stop his crimes. We have considered everything. He is insensitive. He does not care if we call him names or shun

him. We have not the strength to fight him.” She sighed. “It is the only way to save my children.”

The discussion was continuing over and around Mrs. Mus and Cricket, and over and above Cricket’s slow protestations.

"But how shall we do it? That's the question," said the mole, having few resources to violence herself.

"Well," said Mr. Mus, taking the brave lead. "We could bite him to death." The cricket shuddered.

"In the first place," said Chief Ant, "the rat can bite harder than ten mice. The other reasons don't matter." The ants all nodded.

"You're right!" cried Cricket. "Give up the idea!"

"But," Chief Ant went on, "perhaps we could all crawl over him while he's asleep and sting him to death." For once not one other ant was seen to nod. The cricket felt weak. Mrs. Mus felt a bit faint, too.

"It's too chancy," said the spider. "But maybe I could spin a web around him while he's sleeping and pin him down."

"Would it be strong enough?" asked Mr. Mus.

"Possibly not," said the spider, "but it's the only thing I know how to do. Besides, I feel responsible since I suggested the idea in the first place."

Mrs. Mus began to cry. "If we can't kill him, my children will die of hunger. Either the snow must melt overnight, or we just have to get rid of him. There is no other way!"

The cricket knew one thing. The snow was not going to melt overnight.

The rat was back before they had finished the meeting. He was swaggering. His face was full of crumbs. He ambled through the mouse sleeping room and tumbled two small mice onto the cold floor, but he took no notice. "They moved the traps! Fools!" he said. "I've got them flummoxed, the dumb oxes! Well, good night." And he fell asleep with the crumbs still on his face, and his feet muddy. And the cricket, staring at the rat's sleeping face, *knew that he was not remorseful!*

Now a terrible chill affected the cricket, through and through. His eyes were cold, his wings were chilled, and his voice was so slow it could scarcely be understood, but he said, "Very well. I may be able to help you." And he left the compound.

The Only Way

THE CRICKET DID NOT SLEEP that night. He crouched, still shivering, in the privacy of his own home, and the weight of life was very heavy, and the time of night was very long.

In the morning it snowed, but by noon it stopped, and while the cricket sat shivering under the house, Simms helped his father shovel a path to the front gate and another from the back door out to the garage. But though the sun appeared, veiled with gray snow-clouds, it was a cold sun and Mr. Silvanus said, "It will be a good month before those snow banks melt." Later in the day the milk truck came through and Mrs. Silvanus baked some fresh bread.

When Simms came in from shoveling snow, he heard the signal. "Cricket calling Simms," came the message. "Cricket calling Simms."

Simms ran to the telegraph key. It was the first time Cricket had called him. It was quite exciting to be thus summoned. "Simms here."

Cricket wasted no time on courteous preliminaries or formalities. "Has it stopped snowing, please?" came Cricket's voice, and the voice was slower than it usually was.

"Yes," tapped Simms rapidly. "It's stopped."

"Will it melt today, do you think?" creaked Cricket a trifle faster.

"No," tapped Simms. "It won't melt. My father says there's too much of it. The sun isn't warm enough."

There was no reply from Cricket, so Simms tapped, "Are you still there?"

"Yes," said Cricket. "I'm still here." And then, after another pause, he said, "I believe we may be able to help each other." And he creaked this so slowly that Simms was a bit irritated. He, himself, was getting quite skillful.

"Help each other?" he tapped. "How?"

"I can help you catch the rat," creaked the cricket.

"Catch the rat," tapped Simms. "How? How can a cricket catch a rat?"

"You will catch him," creaked Cricket.

"But how can I catch him?" asked Simms. "Even my father hasn't been able to catch him."

"I will tell you where to put the trap," said Cricket. And then he said, "You see, it is necessary in order to save the mouse family. It is the only way." He needed to explain to Simms. "It's the only way for them. And as for you, when you catch the rat your father will be very pleased." Cricket seemed to feel Simms needed to be convinced. "And then, perhaps he will pay more attention to your ideas in the future," added the cricket shrewdly. And this was quite extraordinary, because crickets are not shrewd.

"Oh gosh," said Simms. "That's great! What shall I do?"

And then, slowly, and with great pain, Cricket told Simms about the tunnel behind the furnace wall. "Put the trap right against the opening of the tunnel," said Cricket. "Do it soon, while the rat is sleeping. That's all." And he said nothing else . . . not even "a very good day."

As soon as Cricket finished talking to Simms, he scuttled across the house and down the wall into the basement. Quickly he hopped behind the furnace and into the tunnel. The rat was sleeping on his pile of rags, and Cricket tried not to look at him as he crawled across the wall to the mouse quarters. They were surprised to see him so early in the day, but again he wasted no time on courteous exchanges.

"I have something to tell you," he said very softly. "You must not—repeat, you must *not*—any of you, try to go out the tunnel door tonight. No matter how hungry you are. Not for anything!" He glanced nervously at the sleeping rat. "Do you understand?"

Mr. Mus looked sharply at Cricket. "What is it?" he said.

"I'd rather not say," said Cricket.

"Come on," said the spider, letting himself down into the conversation. "What is it?"

"A trap," said Cricket, with difficulty.

"Where? How? Who?" asked the spider and Mr. Mus.

"No," said Cricket. "It is enough just for me to know." And what he really meant was that it was *too much.*

Beneath the sun porch, the animals retired early, quietly, and without much conversation. The rat lay sleeping loudly, as usual, right up until the moment when he would go out on his night's raid. The mole dozed, but lightly. The spider was restless in his web. The ants were busy in their apartments and not to be seen.

Then, suddenly, one of the Mus offspring leaped out of his bed and started running in the direction of the tunnel.

"No!" cried Mrs. Mus, and she jumped up and started after him. Mr. Mus was ahead of her in a flash of fur and grabbed his son by the tail.

"Where were you going?" he shouted, holding the young Mus tightly, deterring his progress.

"To look for some food for the family," panted Young Mus. "I could climb over that rat without waking him up. I know I could."

Mrs. Mus began to cry and Mr. Mus gave the young Mus his most serious and commanding look. "Get back to bed," he ordered. "You might have been killed!"

"Killed!" came a grating voice from the tunnel entrance. The rat was awake. "Who was killed?"

The Musses were stopped in their tracks as if by an enchantment. The spider said, "There goes the show!"

But Mr. Mus pulled himself together and said with dignity, "We were having a private conversation. Kindly do not interrupt." Then he turned to Mrs. Mus and Young Mus. "Let's go to sleep now. One gets tired early without food."

"But that's why I . . ." Young Mus began.

"Enough!" shouted Mr. Mus, and pushed his family in front of him all the way back to their quarters.

The rat, now fully awake, stretched, yawned, shook himself and looked sullenly around the compound. All eyes were on him. "What are you staring at?" he asked. "Well, what is it? What are you staring at?"

"Nothing," said the spider, who could afford a little back talk from his spot high on the wall. "Just at you . . . and that is at nothing."

"Hush!" said Mrs. Mus warningly, and the rat gave a snarl and leapt up the wall, making a half-hearted swipe at the spider's web, tearing a piece of it. Then he shook himself again and paced around a bit, while everyone continued to stare in silence.

"Ach!" he finally said. "This place is stupid. I'm going to get myself a good meal," and he slunk toward the tunnel.

Everyone heard the snap when it came. And when it came, it was terrible — like a whip is terrible, like a falling tree is terrible, like an ocean storm is terrible . . . like a trap is terrible.

Mr. Mus said "Ah!" but not with satisfaction . . . with resignation. Mrs. Mus screamed. The ants all shook their heads. The mole, who had been dozing, was awake at once and held her breath a bit. The spider, mending the torn web, dropped a stitch, and when that web was finished, one could always see at what point the rattrap snapped.

And underneath Simms' room, the cricket heard it and for the first time in his life he wept. Crickets shed no tears actually, so it was not with his eyes that he wept, nor chokingly in his throat, nor snufflingly, exactly. But still, unmistakably, he cried. For a habitually cheerful creature, it was a hard experience.

He was quite exhausted when he finally stopped, and not relieved nor renewed as one sometimes is by a good weep. He was weary, longing for warm sun, cool grass . . . and longing, yes, longing, for his love.

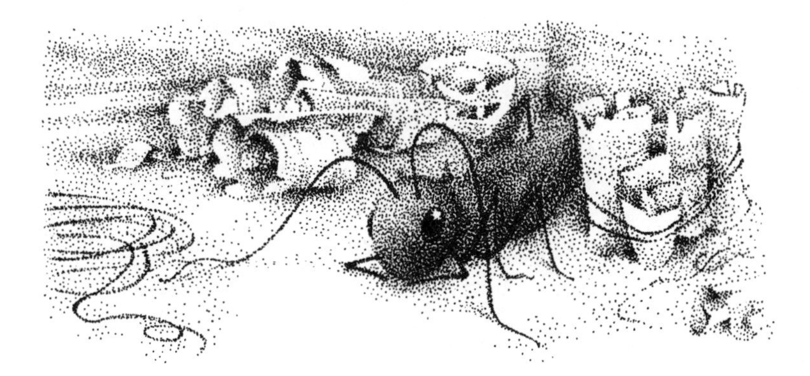

That's Everything

THE LONGEST NIGHT OF THE YEAR was the night the rat was killed. It does not matter what the calendar says. The boy slept fitfully, impatient to inspect his trap and win the approval of his father. And the cricket . . . oh, for the cricket, sleepless again, torn with sadness, the night seemed not to end. And yet, toward morning he dozed, and then was awakened by a familiar sound.

"Simms here! Simms here," came the rapidly repeated tapping of the telegraph key. "Calling Cricket. Calling Cricket. Simms here."

Cricket shook his head, trying to get the feel of the time and place, and then he creaked, "Cricket here."

"We caught him," Simms tapped, and the rapidity of the message gave a clue to his excitement. "We caught him. I've just given him a sort of funeral."

"Ah!" said the cricket. "You did well. Very well. There was no other way, you know."

"I know," said Simms.

"What did your father say?" asked Cricket. "Did he praise you?"

"He left the house before I could tell him," said Simms, and then he frowned and said, "but there's an awful problem about that."

"Oh dear," creaked Cricket. "What kind of a problem?"

"Well," tapped Simms, "of course, I was planning to tell him just as soon as he comes home, but I'm afraid now he will want to know *where* I set the trap. And if I tell him where I set the trap, he will . . . ."

Cricket was beginning to see the problem. He had not thought of it himself. Boys are more foresighted than crickets.

"You mean," Cricket chirped cautiously, "he might set more traps there and catch the *mice*?"

"Yes," said Simms. "Or he might even plug up the hole. I don't know what to do. It's a hard problem."

"Yes," agreed Cricket. "It is a hard problem."

"My father isn't going to like mice very much either, you see."

"No," said Cricket, and he knew very well — better than most — that only one person can decide hard problems such as this.

"And I do want him to know it was I who caught the rat," tapped Simms.

"Yes," agreed Cricket. "It would be nice. That was one of the ideas, of course."

"But if I tell him . . . *Well, I just can't,* that's all! I can't tell him."

For the first time in many hours the cricket felt the glimmer of a fine good feeling returning to him under his crisp little chitin coat. He chirped more quickly now. "I believe you are doing the right thing," he said.

"You do?" asked Simms.

"Yes, I do, truly," chirped Cricket. "It is a hard thing, but it feels right."

"It feels right to me, too," said Simms.

All the optimism that is part of being a cricket now came back to Cricket. He felt just as he did the day he first saw the sky. His voice was clear when he chirped, "Simms, how are things?"

"Quite good," tapped Simms, "considering."

"That's fine," said Cricket. "Tell me, do you

have . . . do you have . . ." Now Cricket's voice trailed off.

"Have what?" tapped Simms.

"Love?" chirped Cricket at last.

Simms wasn't sure he had heard the message correctly. "Repeat, please," he tapped.

The cricket's voice was soft. "Love," he chirped. "Do you have love?"

Simms laughed, and then he grew serious for a moment before he answered. No one had ever asked him that before. He thought about it. He thought about his mother and he thought about his father, his grandmother, his grandfather, his friends . . . and then he said, "I guess so. Yes, I guess I do."

"Oh, that's good!" chirped Cricket. "That's very good. Simms, I wonder if I could ask you to send a message for me? I want very much . . .very much to send a message to . . . to a friend. Could you do it?"

"I could do my best," said Simms, "but I don't know. You see I can't send messages very long distances. Where is your friend?"

"In your garage loft," said Cricket.

"Oh, that's all right then," tapped Simms. "What shall I say?"

"Say this," said Cricket, and he proceeded to chirp out a message that was completely incomprehensible to Simms.

"Sorry," tapped Simms. "I must have got the code mixed up. I don't get the words. Repeat, please."

"It's not in your language," said Cricket. "Could you just remember the way the signals go and copy them? They're not people words . . . they're cricket words."

"Oh," said Simms. "All right. Go ahead, but go slowly." And while the cricket chirped a message

to his love, Simms committed it to memory.

"If she replies," said Cricket, "and she probably won't, could you remember what she says? Please."

"All right," said Simms. "I'd better go now while I remember it," and he ran down the newly shoveled path to the garage.

He climbed the narrow ladder to the garage loft, and standing on the top rung, he looked around at the old bicycle tires, shovel handles, and empty paint cans. There was not a creature to be seen. He took his telegraph key out of his pocket and laid it on the floor of the loft. Then, very carefully, he

tapped out Cricket's message.

After that, there was not a sound except the wind blowing the snow on the roof. And then, from a far corner of the attic, came a very faint, slowly chirped reply.

Simms was ready. He remembered every chirp and ran back to the house.

"Message for Cricket," he tapped.

"Go ahead, please," chirped Cricket.

"Her message is just the same as yours," said Simms. "Just exactly the same!"

Joy flooded Cricket. There was a resurgence, now, of the complete delight of being a cricket. He said, "Thank you. Thank you, Simms."

"Is there anything else?"

"No," said Cricket. "*That's everything.*"

A cricket is a delicate creature — one of the poetic things that nature has worked out — and a cricket-in-love is so tender and heartrending, so attuned to his love, that he is, for the moment, at least, quite perfect.

A boy of nine is enormously wise and has a great deal to tell, if anyone at all would listen. And yet it is a fact that the ideas and opinions of many boys of nine go with very little notice or are entirely overlooked. Many adults who could learn from them, if they would, pass them by in a great hurry. It is not a perfect situation.

But, just once in a while, a boy may do a fine thing and get no recognition at all, and it's all right. It's enough. Indeed, he feels, for the moment, quite perfect.

Acknowledgments

I thank Anna Marlis Burgard of Design Press at the Savannah College of Art and Design for selecting *The Cricket Winter* for this new edition, and for her sensitive artistic and editorial direction throughout. From here, every step has been a pleasure.

And thanks to Marcia Kelly for introducing us in the first place.

A special thank you to Robyn Thomas for bringing Cricket back to chirp again. Crickets are lucky and I hope ours brings her much success.

—F. H.